State Rebellion:

A PLAN FOR FIGHTING THE REDCOATS IN WASHINGTON, DC

By Michael Warren

Righter Books

Copyright 2015 by Michael Warren
All rights reserved

No part of this book may be reproduced without written permission by the author.

Righter Publishing Company, Inc.
1112 Rogers Road
Graham, North Carolina 27253

www.righterbooks.com

First Edition
June 2015

Printed and bound in the United States of America

ISBN: 978-1-938527-28-9
State Rebellion
By Michael Warren

Also available at Amazon Kindle

"Government is not reason. It is not eloquence—it is a force! Like fire, it is a dangerous servant and a fearful master; never for a moment should it be left to irresponsible action."

George Washington, Eleventh President of the United States

"If in the opinion of the People, the distribution or modification of the Constitutional powers be in any particular wrong, let it be corrected by an amendment in the way which the Constitution designates. But let there be no change by usurpation; for though this, in one instance, may be the instrument of good, it is the customary weapon by which free governments are destroyed."

George Washington

Farewell Address, September 19, 1796

THE FIRST ELEVEN U.S. PRESIDENTS

(The Articles Of Confederation were ratified by Maryland on March 1, 1781, making the sitting President of the Continental Congress the first President of the United States In Congress Assembled.)

Samuel Huntington
March 1, 1781 to July 6, 1781

Thomas McKean
July 10, 1781 to November 5, 1781

John Hanson
November 5, 1781 to November 4, 1782

Elias Boudinot
November 4, 1782 to November 3, 1783

Thomas Mifflin
November 3, 1783 to June 3, 1784

Richard Henry Lee
November 30, 1784 to November 23, 1785

John Hancock
November 23, 1785 to June 6, 1786

Nathaniel Gorham
June 6, 1786 to November 13, 1786

Arthur St. Clair
February 2, 1787 to October 29, 1787

Cyrus Griffin
January 22, 1788 to March 4, 1789

George Washington
April 30, 1789 to March 4, 1793

Table of Contents

INTRODUCTION 8

PRINCIPLES OF AMERICAN CONSTITUTIONAL FEDERALISM 11

PATRICK HENRY'S RATS: THE ADVENT OF NATIONALIST GOVERNMENT 14

NECESSITY OF FEDERAL GOVERNANCE BY THE STATES 17

THE ENGLISH NATIONAL GOVERNMENT IN THE COLONIES 24

THE FRAMERS REJECT A NATIONALIST GOVERNMENT 27

THE NATIONALIST STRATEGY: USURPATION 31

USURPATION ONE JOHN MARSHALL: CREATION OF THE NATIONALIST JUDICIARY 33

USURPATION TWO ABRAHAM LINCOLN: CREATION OF THE NATIONALIST UNION 43

USURPATION THREE WOODROW WILSON: CREATION OF THE NATIONALIST EXECUTIVE 48

USURPATION FOUR FRANKLIN DELANO ROOSEVELT: CREATION OF THE NATIONALIST LEGISLATURE 52

USURPATION FIVE THE FEDERAL RESERVE: CREATION OF THE NATIONALIST ECONOMY 56

THE CONSTITUTIONAL IMPERATIVE 62

THE PALMETTO MANIFESTO 64

Summary Of The Palmetto Manifesto 65

ARTICLE 1: Federal Power Permanently Restrained 69

ARTICLE 2: Super-majority Of States May Renounce Any Federal Action 74

ARTICLE 3: States To Collect Federal Tax Defined In Constitution 79

ARTICLE 4: Senators Appointed By State Legislatures ... 86

ARTICLE 5: Abolition Of Income Tax 89

ARTICLE 6: President Must First Be Governor 92

ARTICLE 7: Senator Must First Be Mayor 94

ARTICLE 8: House Member Must First Be County Commissioner 96

ARTICLE 9: Supreme Court Justice Must First Be Magistrate 98

ARTICLE 10: War Powers Returned To States 102

ARTICLE 11: Members Of Congress To Serve Single Term 106

ARTICLE 12: Congress Members May Serve In One House Only 108

ARTICLE 13: Members Of Congress Excluded From Cabinet 110

ARTICLE 14: Cabinet Excluded From Congress 112

ARTICLE 15: Ambassador Must First Be Secretary Of State In A State 114

ARTICLE 16: President Must Be Born In A State 116

ARTICLE 17: Treaty Inferior To US Law 118

ARTICLE 18: Birth Citizenship Restricted To Children Of US Citizens 120

ARTICLE 19: Legal Entry Required For Immigrant Citizenship 123

ARTICLE 20: Return To Gold Standard 125

ARTICLE 21: Hate Speech Protected 127

ARTICLE 22: Withdrawal From The United Nations 129

ARTICLE 23: Abolition Of Federal Education 131

ARTICLE 24: Commerce Clause Restricted 135

ARTICLE 25: Volunteer Service Abolished And Universal Conscription Established 139

INTRODUCTION

As the Philadelphia Convention adjourned on September 17, 1787, the wife of the mayor of Philadelphia asked Benjamin Franklin what kind of new government had been created. Franklin answered, "A republic, madam. If you can keep it."

Little did the lady know that Redcoats, former crown loyalists who had been vanquished by the Revolution, were still willing to fight for what they truly wanted: a national government for America. With the British Army defeated and sent back to England, the Redcoats could no longer hope for the king to rule the colonies.

But they could aspire to have all the powers of government vested in a central government, a national government that would rule the unruly States. No longer able to fly the Union Jack as their banner, no longer able to command armies in the field, the Redcoats switched tactics. First they tried to persuade the delegates at the Philadelphia Convention to adopt a national government in their new constitution.

The idea of a national government was soundly rejected by the delegates. Instead they fashioned a federal government with powers shared between powerful State governments and a central government with expressly delegated, carefully enumerated powers. Though the Redcoats had been defeated again, they did not give up.

Once again, they switched tactics. They decided they could achieve their objective of a national government by usurpation. They would gradually steal power from State governments and thus expand the national government beyond the federal bounds prescribed by the Constitution. In this, the Redcoats have very nearly succeeded. Fashion changes with time. The Redcoats no longer wear red coats and they prefer to be called nationalists. But we shall see that the leopard cannot change its spots. We shall take a brief look at history and we shall see the Redcoats, moving stealthily in the grass, ready to pounce upon the weakened body of our constitutionally federated government.

Even learned historians are reluctant to accept that the greatest Redcoat marauders of our Constitution are Chief Justice John Marshall, President Lincoln, President Wilson, President Franklin Delano Roosevelt and, once again, President Franklin Delano Roosevelt.

This book identifies the tactics of the five great usurpers for imposing a nationalist government on the States. As a remedy, it presents the Palmetto Manifesto, twenty-five proposed individual amendments to the Constitution which, if adopted, will restore the supreme political authority of the States and permanently restrain federal power.

As President Washington suggested, the fight against usurpation should be accomplished with individual amendments, not with revolution. As happened in 1787 in Philadelphia, a constitutional convention would fail because it would soon be taken over by special interests. State rebellion, a legislative war prescribed by the Palmetto Manifesto, will take down the Redcoat government already operating in Washington, DC.

PRINCIPLES OF AMERICAN CONSTITUTIONAL FEDERALISM

1. The word "federal" comes from the Latin "foedus" which means league, treaty, or compact. States—free, independent, deliberate bodies politic in confederation—is the only form of government created by the Constitution of 1787. The confederation was created by the legislatures in the States, not by the people in the States. Only the legislatures of the States are parties to the Constitution; the central government they created is subject to, but not a party to, the Constitution.

2. The Constitution is not statute law; it is not common law; it is not a treaty; it is not a contract. The Constitution is an express compact among sovereign States.

3. America is not a nation and it is not an amalgam of people; it is a deliberate confederation of consenting bodies politic known as States. America did not begin as a nation and to this very day it has never, by virtue of authority or Constitution or law, consented to be a nation. Americans have never agreed to be governed by a single authority. Americans have never legally formed a nationalist government. Despite this, our federal government has usurped the powers of, and has come to operate as, a nationalist government.

4. Political authority is the moral legitimacy which allows one deliberative body to make binding laws for their peers. Political power is simply the ability of one body to enforce its will on others. The only political authority in America belongs to the States. This authority was won by revolution, at a cost of 4,435 lives. When the legislatures of the States created the federal government to serve them, they conferred on the central government limited powers but they gave it no political authority. The States retain all political authority in America. Since political authority precedes and is superior to political power, the State legislatures are the final arbiters of federal power. The State legislatures must actively govern all exercises of power by the federal government which they alone created, for which they alone are responsible, and which only they may change or abolish.

5. The federal government exists only as a creature of the States. The legislatures of the States, and not the people in the States, created the federal government via constitution and ratification. As a creature of the States, the federal government has no political authority whatsoever and is subservient to the will of the States. Thus, the States, by due process in the States, may rescind, nullify, void, cancel and halt enforcement of any law, regulation, judicial decision, executive order, declaration of war, treaty or any provision thereof, contract, arbitration, or any other act or commitment of any branch, department, agency, committee, commission, delegation,

ambassador or any person, agent, corporation or entity of any kind operating under the custom, color, authority, instruction, capacity or will of the federal government.

6. The American federal republic will not survive unless the legislatures in the States immediately begin, by the process of individual constitutional amendment, to govern the exercise of power by the federal government and establish themselves, in the Constitution, as the final arbiters of federal power.

7. The federal government has no political authority. It has only the limited powers conferred on it by the States. Because it has no political authority, any exercise of power by the federal government which was not granted to it by the States, is illegal and unconstitutional and must be resisted by all legal citizens in the States. If such an illegal exercise of power by the federal government usurps the powers of the States, such exercise of power is treason and must be resisted, opposed and countermanded by both the legislatures of the States and all legal citizens in the States.

PATRICK HENRY'S RATS: THE ADVENT OF NATIONALIST GOVERNMENT

When Patrick Henry was asked why he boycotted the Philadelphia Convention of 1787, he replied that he "smelt a rat." He was right to be concerned. The delegates to that convention were charged by their State legislatures with revising the existing constitution, the Articles Of Confederation. Yet, the first two things decided by the convention were to operate in secrecy and to scrap the Articles and write a new constitution.

Henry, a staunch defender of the Articles of Confederation, feared that the delegates to the convention were fomenting a second revolution, a coup against freedoms newly won. "Revolutions like this have happened in almost every country in Europe: similar examples are to be found in ancient Greece and ancient Rome: instances of the people losing their liberty by their own carelessness and the ambitions of a few."

Henry was convinced that those who had already benefitted from the consolidated government brought about by the Articles Of Confederation simply wanted to increase their power. Henry would not take part in such usurpation and he cautioned: "You are not to inquire how your trade may be increased, nor how you are to become a great and prosperous people, but how your liberties can be secured, for liberty ought to be the end of your government."

Our celebrated current constitution began as a usurpation of power by the delegates to the Philadelphia Convention. They did however listen to Henry's advice as they fashioned in secrecy, heedless of their charter, a new government. Perhaps because they themselves were usurpers, the rats at the Philadelphia Convention neglected to put anti-usurpation provisions to restrain the new government they illegitimately created. Patrick Henry's rats unwittingly left the constitutional door ajar and since 1787 other political rats have been gnawing on the principles of liberty that were originally constituted for the American people by the Philadelphia rats. Greatest among the usurping rats who followed Henry's rats were Chief Justice John Marshall in 1803, President Abraham Lincoln in 1861, President Woodrow Wilson in 1914, President Franklin Roosevelt in 1933, and President Franklin Roosevelt, a rat with an enormous appetite, again in 1935.

These five great usurping rats have brought us perilously close to nationalist government in America. Nationalist government in America occurs when the States are eliminated as political entities and the resulting government has all political power. The existence of the States with their constitutional powers is the single component of governance that makes our government federal. A federal government is what Henry's rats crafted at the Philadelphia

Convention. The Framers specifically prohibited in the new U.S. constitution: a national government. Their constitution authorizes only a federal government. Therefore, a nationalist government would be a ROGUE government because it would be unconstitutional and thus both lawless and unlimited. Unlimited lawlessness is certainly the political collapse of a republic.

      This book details the work of the Five Great Usurpers and explains how their travesties have brought us to the very edge of nationalist government in America. It provides a step-by-step, comprehensive plan to redistribute governance back to the States and permanently seal the Framers' loophole that has allowed the republic to peacefully approach extinction.

NECESSITY OF FEDERAL GOVERNANCE BY THE STATES

"To take a single step beyond the boundaries [of the Constitution] is to take possession of a boundless field of power, no longer susceptible to any definition."

Thomas Jefferson, 1791

The federal republic created by the States via the Constitution has been methodically sabotaged and usurped by political forces seeking to impose a nationalist government on those States. This movement to dissolve the constitutionally federated government and replace it with a nationalist government holding all power has nearly succeeded in destroying the only source of valid political authority in the United States: the States themselves. Now, once again, as anticipated by Thomas Jefferson, rebellion is necessary.

The principle underlying the constitution that replaced the Articles Of Confederation was that the State legislatures would actively govern the central power they had created to serve them. Indeed, the Framers established an intra-federal system of checks and balances to regulate the central government. The grave error made by the Framers was the failure to specify in the Constitution an extra-federal restraint on the central government to prevent expansion of federal power by the collusion of the branches of the federal government.

Constitutional federal government in America, and thus the Republic itself, has been subject to a massive subversion by colluding branches of the central government because of the Seven Deadly Sins Of The States at the Philadelphia Convention:

Sin 1: The States did not permanently constrain federal political power by making the entire federal government subject to a super majority of State legislatures.

Sin 2: The States did not permanently constrain federal taxing power by making federal taxing power subject to a super majority of State legislatures.

Sin 3: The States did not permanently constrain federal war power by making the federal war power subject to a super majority of State legislatures.

Sin 4: The States did not permanently constrain federal political careers by setting term limits and requiring relevant experience.

Sin 5: The States did not permanently constrain federal citizenship power by defining citizens.

Sin 6: The States did not permanently constrain federal economic power by requiring the federal government to have a vested interest in the prosperity of the economies of the States.

Sin 7: The States did not permanently constrain federal cultural power by forbidding federal government control of education.

These failures by the States have resulted in the people having been overwhelmed by the statist regime imposed on them by the Republicans, Democrats and other political parties. The people cannot now bring about the required rebellion. Force of arms cannot bring about the required rebellion. Rebellion must begin now against our rogue nationalist government and it must be accomplished by our State legislatures through the power of individual constitutional amendments.

State legislatures, not the people, created the federal government to serve those legislatures. The States, the only entities possessing original political authority, have neglected to restrain the federal monster they fashioned. Now, the States must rebel or the States, which truly are the Republic, will die!

Because the Redcoat government in Washington, DC is exercising unconstitutional powers, it is a rogue government, not a true government. As it is a rogue, the government must be opposed and resisted by all citizens of the United States in the only way this government of nationalist usurpation can be repelled by convincing their State legislatures to propose and to ratify Constitutional amendments to redistribute government back to the States. The States must govern the federal power they created.

The Palmetto Manifesto organizes the necessary amendments that will restore and permanently constrain a constitutionally federated government. This rebellious program is named after the freedom firebrand State of South Carolina. May the State of South Carolina—the State that saved the Revolution, the State that revolted to save the Constitution—be the first State to rebel by being the first to introduce into Congress the proposed amendments of the Palmetto Manifesto and the first to fight for their adoption.

Until now, the States, which created the federal government to serve them, have not acted to restrain the nationalist autocracy and restore our federal government. Unless they act quickly and decisively, the States will disappear as political powers. If the States are totally usurped, a violent revolution would then be necessary to destroy the government of nationalist usurpation.

A nationalist government is a government with unlimited power that rules an entire nation and is answerable only to itself. No such government has been legal in America since the Revolution. Government officials in Washington, DC blatantly ignore this historical fact. They do so at their peril. They are rogues and must be treated as such.

The U.S. Constitution established a federal government, with limited powers, to serve the State governments that created it. Under our American constitution, a nationalist government is explicitly forbidden and expressly illegal. When the Framers were explaining the new government they had wrought during the ratifying conventions in the States, they assured the people that their new constitution would establish a federal government with limited, enumerated powers. They had not, they promised, fashioned a nationalist government for America.

Patrick Henry did not believe them and became a passionate Anti-Federalist. The Framers, themselves usurpers against the Articles Of Confederation, although they did not intentionally create a nationalist government, by omission, did make such a government possible.

Yet, our so-called federal government, before the ink had dried on the ratified Constitution, and with the indulgence of the State governments that created it, began assuming the powers of a nationalist government. The system of federal checks and balances failed almost immediately because these constitutional restraints on power were designed as intra-federal measures which each branch of the government would enforce to protect its own power against the others. In the face of inexplicably timid State legislatures, and without an extra-federal constraint to bind them, each branch of the federal government constantly usurped power from the States.

Unfortunately, the Framers did not include in the Constitution the extra-federal restriction that would have precluded the branches of the federal government from stealing power from the States and the people. Had the Framers explicitly stated the supremacy of the State legislatures over the federal government, they would have closed the door to the expansion of central government power.

The government now sitting in Washington, DC has far exceeded the powers delegated to it by its constitutional charter, therefore it is a rogue nationalist government. This unconscionable, self-aggrandizing government must be reined in permanently by those who created it, the legislatures of the States.

"When the representative body have lost the confidence of their constituents, when they have notoriously made sale of their most valuable rights, when they have assumed to themselves powers which the people never put into their hands, then indeed their continuing in office becomes dangerous to the state and calls for an exercise of the power of dissolution."

Thomas Jefferson, A Summary View Of The Rights Of British America

The Palmetto Manifesto outlined in this book offers proposed constitutional amendments that will break the back of the rogue Redcoat government in Washington, DC, re-establish the supremacy of the State legislatures, restore the meaning of the Constitution and enshrine a federal republic for the United States of America in perpetuity.

The people of the colonies prevailed against King George III, the people of the Confederate States preserved their honor against King Lincoln, and the people of the United States will, by adopting the Palmetto Manifesto herein described, depose kingly government in America, once and for all. This final act of defiance will unequivocally mark the U.S. Constitution as the foundation of a dependent federal government which serves at the will of the sovereign States that created it and rule it.

With the publication of the Palmetto Manifesto, the fall of Washington, and its rogue Redcoat government, will have begun. May it come with all deliberate speed, withering nationalistic ambitions, root and branch. Patrick Henry's rats have been very busy since 1787. The time has come to kill them, once and for all, with the Palmetto Manifesto. State rebellion it is, in just measure, just in the nick of time to save the Republic.

THE ENGLISH NATIONAL GOVERNMENT IN THE COLONIES

The English crown established a national government for its colonies in America. This crown government had unlimited power and ruled everyone in the colonies. Even though the London Company, which had received the patent from King James I for the Jamestown, Virginia settlement established in 1607, had given these first English settlers the right to make their own laws in the Great Charter of 1613, the settlers at Plymouth Rock, before they ever reached the American shore, gave this right to themselves.

Therefore, initial opposition to the national crown government in America did not begin with a gunshot in Lexington, Massachusetts Bay colony, on April 19, 1775; it began off the coast of Cape Cod on November 11, 1620. Adopted on that date, the Mayflower Compact did not prescribe law: it created the original authority for all law in the English domain of America. This brief agreement, to which the crown was not a party, created the first independent consenting body politic in America.

The political authority the people gave themselves on that day would prove superior to the laws of the national government and would ultimately deny the crown its colonies. This should not have surprised the English, for their own history demonstrates that before any entity may prescribe law, it must first obtain the authority to do so. The Mayflower Compact established that the crown did not have the authority to create a national government for America.

In 1624, King James revoked the Great Charter of 1613 and issued a new one in which the settlers in Virginia could make their own laws but the King would appoint their council and their governor. This act made Virginia a royal province and therefore the body politic in Virginia lost its brief independence but the crown lost its authority—though not its power—to make laws for Virginia. This loss of authority for the crown would soon spread to the other colonies.

In 1776, the American colonies seceded from the national government of the crown and fought a war to secure their freedom and independence from that national government. When King George III signed the Treaty of Paris in 1783 to end his war with his former colonies, he did not recognize and accept the freedom of a new nation, he acknowledged the independence of 13 nations, and he took the trouble, lest there be doubt, to name them:

"His Britannic Majesty acknowledges the said United States, viz., New Hampshire, Massachusetts Bay, Rhode Island and Providence Plantations, Connecticut, New York, New Jersey, Pennsylvania, Delaware, Maryland, Virginia, North Carolina, South Carolina, and Georgia to be free, sovereign and independent States…"

The word "state", in the eighteenth century, meant nation. George III's signature made these 13 nations free, independent and sovereign as a matter of law. The English experiment with a national government in America was over.

So when you hear the President pontificating about a "national problem" or some bombastic member of Congress bragging about creating a "national solution", remember this: America is not a nation, it is a deliberate confederation of States formed after those States, at a cost of 4,435 killed in battle, rid themselves of the national government the British crown had imposed on them.

THE FRAMERS REJECT A NATIONALIST GOVERNMENT

"Each State in ratifying the Constitution, is considered as a sovereign body independent of all others, and only to be bound by its own voluntary act. In this relation then the new Constitution, if established, be a *federal* and not a *national* Constitution."

James Madison, Federalist Essay No. 39
January 16, 1788

When the Philadelphia Convention opened its deliberations at the Pennsylvania State House, later known as Independence Hall, in May of 1787, the purported reason for the assembly was to draft amendments remedying defects in the Articles Of Confederation. However, the first point the delegates agreed to—after they had already committed to operating in secrecy—was that the Confederation would be scrapped and they would create a new central government with a legislature, a judiciary and an executive.

This motive of usurpation was the reason Patrick Henry claimed he "smelt a rat" and did not attend the meeting. From the beginning, the Philadelphia Convention contravened the express purpose for which their respective States, Rhode Island excepted, had authorized the delegates to meet.

Although the Convention did debate two approaches to forming a new government, known as the Virginia Plan and the New Jersey Plan, the latter was dispensed with quickly. The Virginia Plan, authored mostly by James Madison, which would have created a powerful nationalist government and denied the States any real authority, was amended from the start to give the new government a federal form. The delegates clearly did not want to create either a monarchy, as Alexander Hamilton favored, or a nationalist government, as the Virginia delegates had originally proposed.

The delegates had been sent by sovereign State governments and they adamantly refused to dissolve the States in favor of a single nationalist government. Even Alexander Hamilton, who hoped to install a nationalist government modeled after Britain, had to admit in 1788, "While this Constitution continues to be read, and its principles known, the states must, by every man, be considered as essential, components parts of the Union."

James Madison's Virginia Plan called for both houses of the bicameral Congress to be based on proportional representation. The delegates recognized that this arrangement would leave all power in the hands of the larger States, and they rejected it. Not only were the delegates determined to create a federal government of the States, they wanted all States to have fair representation in the new government. Roger Sherman of Connecticut fashioned a compromise in which representation in the House would be based on population and the representation in the Senate would be equal for all States.

To their credit, the delegates to the Philadelphia Convention rejected the aristocratic sentiments of their high-born members, did not establish a monarchy and refused to create a nationalist government. They were representing sovereign States, States who had won their independence through war. These learned men had the courage to preserve their sacred State governments by fashioning, as an assistant to those State governments, a strictly limited federal government. Precisely because of the esteem the delegates had for their State constitutions, and their knowledge that their basic rights were already protected by their State constitutions, they refused to include a Bill Of Rights in the new Constitution. Though these rights were added later as the first ten amendments, to protect those territories who had no constitutions because they were not yet States, they were not a part of the original Constitution. The rights of the Framers were guaranteed by their States.

The Convention did not accept a nationalist government. The Convention rejected the idea that Congress should be able to veto State laws; it dismissed Hamilton's notion that the President should appoint State governors and State senators; it refused Madison's concept that Congress should have a general legislative power; it did not allow federal courts to have a general jurisdiction; it enumerated the powers given to the central government and explicitly reserved remaining powers to the States and the people.

THE NATIONALIST STRATEGY: USURPATION

Patrick Henry had correctly sensed the intentions of the delegates who met at the Philadelphia Convention: usurpation of power. They had been authorized only to revise the Articles Of Confederation yet they took it upon themselves to seize a power not given to them: they created a new constitution. Unfortunately, this appetite for usurpation infected the new government they created.

The fact that the Philadelphia Convention adopted on September 17, 1787, a constitution for a federal government did not prevent the newly established central government from trying to appropriate the power of a nationalist government. From the moment the State legislatures created the federal republic by ratifying the Constitution on June 21, 1788, the Legislative branch, the Executive branch and the Judicial branch have consistently, continually and unconstitutionally sought to seize powers not granted them. The goal of this usurpation is the unlawful establishment of a nationalist government by the removal of all significant power from the State governments. Such a rogue Redcoat government would hold all power and be answerable only to itself.

The nationalist strategy of usurpation was possible because, although the Framers brilliantly designed intra-federal checks and balances and separations of powers, they failed to include in the Constitution the explicit extra-federal check that the legislatures of the States were the final arbiters of all federal power. The lack of this supreme extra-federal check meant that each branch of the federal government, by supporting the usurpation of the other branches, could grow its own power and eventually surpass all constitutional bounds.

A comprehensive nationalist usurpation has come to pass through the ambitions of the Five Great Usurpers: John Marshall, Abraham Lincoln, Woodrow Wilson, Franklin Delano Roosevelt once and FDR once again. Today, America is governed by an illegal, unconstitutional rogue Redcoat government. This government should be brought down and this book demonstrates the necessary plan of attack.

USURPATION ONE
JOHN MARSHALL:
CREATION OF THE NATIONALIST JUDICIARY

"It is emphatically the duty of the Judicial Department to say what the law is."

Chief Justice John Marshall, Marbury v. Madison, 1803

The American colonies were chartered as corporations, so in the colonial experience of the Framers, judicial review was common. After the Revolution, this review occurred in State courts as examinations of State law against State constitutions. As it was not new to them, the Framers did not discuss judicial review in the Philadelphia Convention and they did not provide for it in the Constitution. Nonetheless, they were accustomed to it.

In 1796, the Supreme Court heard the case of Hylton v. United States. At issue was whether or not a 1794 Congressional tax on carriages was a direct tax, in violation of the Constitution. Incredibly, the Court ruled that the carriage tax was not a direct tax. The remarkable thing about this decision is the Court's view of judicial review and the Court's understanding of the Constitution.

"....it is unnecessary, at this time, for me to determine whether this court, constitutionally possesses the power to declare an act of Congress void...."

Justice Samuel Chase

The Court was not yet ready to assert that it could void an act of Congress, but its view of the Constitution, only a few years old, opened the door to the flood of judicial usurpation that would follow.

"The Constitution has been considered as an accommodating system; it was the effect of mutual sacrifices and concessions; it was the work of compromise."

Justice William Patterson

What is striking about Patterson's statement is that though the Constitution was the result of wrangling in deliberation, the resulting document was a compact of carefully chosen, fixed meaning. By whom was it considered "accommodating"? The Framers did not have that view; the defenders of the proposed Constitution did not represent that view to the ratifying conventions they addressed, and the conventions did not express that view as the Constitution was ratified. If the Constitution had been described as accommodating to central government power rather than strictly limiting central government power, no State would have ratified it.

There were opponents to a federal government in the days after the Revolution. Some wanted to establish a monarchy for America—an offer was made to Prince Henry of Prussia but was revoked before he could reply. Others wanted a powerful nationalist government. Such ambitions had been thwarted in Philadelphia by the creation of a federal constitution.

An indirect path to a nationalist, unconstitutional government lay open through interpretation, rather than application, of the provisions of the Constitution. Justice Patterson started the country down that path, but it was Chief Justice John Marshall who ran a freight train in that unwarranted direction.

The newly created Supreme Court did not possess prestige as did the Congress and the President. When John Marshall became Chief Justice in 1801, he was determined to garner some glory for the Court. He got his chance in 1803 in the case of Marbury v Madison.

Marshall, had he been a man of integrity, would have recused himself from the case. His dereliction of duty, as Secretary of State for outgoing President John Adams, had caused this case to arise, as he knew it would—just as he knew that outgoing President John Adams would appoint him Chief Justice.

Ambition, rather than character ruled Marshall. He created this case for a court he knew he would lead and for a purpose to which all branches of the new federal government were dedicated: using the unchecked court to expand their power beyond its constitutional limits. Marshall was only too glad to lead the federal charge through this constitutional loophole. After all, being the grand marshal of the federal usurpation parade allowed him to garner prestige for his overshadowed court, and himself in the bargain.

As he was leaving office, and just before his party lost control of Congress, President John Adams had appointed multiple judges. At the time, they were called "midnight judges". These judges were approved by the Senate and their commissions were signed by the President. To become effective, these commissions had to be delivered to the recipients by the Secretary of State John Marshall.

Marshall did not deliver some of the commissions. President John Adams then appointed Marshall Chief Justice. The incoming President Jefferson voided the undelivered commissions because they had not been properly handled. William Marbury then sued the new Secretary of State, James Madison, seeking to force Madison to deliver his commission. Compelling Madison to forward the commission to Marbury involved a new judiciary act passed by Congress.

Marshall had his chance to assert judicial review of his court over the will of Congress. In writing the decision, Marshall asserted, "It is emphatically the duty of the Judicial Department to say what the law is." He further declared, "....a law repugnant to the Constitution is void...."

Marshall's ruling implies, but does not state, that only the Supreme Court can say what the law is and what is repugnant to the Constitution. The Constitution does not give or prohibit this power. Federal review of a federal law still leaves the supreme judiciary operating as a federal judiciary, but Marshall soon had his chance to make the Supreme Court a nationalist judiciary, an entity not formulated in the Constitution.

The Philadelphia Convention considered but rejected a proposal to give Congress the power to veto the acts of State legislatures. The ratified Constitution also did not give this power to the Supreme Court. In 1810, in the case of Fletcher v. Peck, the Court gave this power to itself. This case involved land speculation in the famous Yazoo land scandal. As he was himself a major land speculator, Marshall should have recused himself but once again, he did not. The Constitution does not give the Supreme Court the power to veto State legislation so Marshall should have dismissed the case out of hand and remanded it to the State courts in Georgia. Instead, he ruled a Georgia law unconstitutional and void.

Now the Court was operating as a nationalist, not a federal judiciary; it would soon set the federal executive branch free to become a national executive and the federal legislative branch free to become a nationalist legislature.

The Court had cracked the door on nationalist tyranny and would soon fling it open with abandon. Damn the Constitution! The era of Manifest National Power had begun! The race was on to see which branch of the old federal government could grab the most nationalist power in the shortest amount of time. George Washington's warning would have been daunting, if anyone had remembered it. Before Mussolini, Hitler and Stalin, the government of America was fervently telling the Big Lie and telling it so often that the people would come to believe it. What was the Big Lie? America is a nation. Not a word of it was true. Every word of it was designed to steal power.

In 1816, the Court was able to extend its nationalist agenda in the case of Martin v. Hunter's Lessee. This case also involved land titles and companies in which John Marshall and his brother were participating. Amazingly, Marshall did recuse himself from this case so Justice Story delivered the opinion.

There should have been no case at all. The Virginia Court Of Appeals refused to deliver the case files to the Supreme Court for review, stating, "The court is unanimously of opinion that the appellate power of the Supreme Court of the United States does not extend to this court, under a sound construction of the Constitution of the United States...."

The Virginia Court of Appeals was correct. The Supreme Court was wrong but abrogated the power to supervise State courts. In setting aside a Virginia law, Justice Story opined that there must be one supreme authority to make sure that the law was applied in the same manner.

Justice Story was correct when he said, "The questions involved in this judgment are of great importance and delicacy. Perhaps it is not too much to affirm that, upon their right decision rest some of the most solid principles which have hitherto been supposed to sustain and protect the Constitution itself."

Unfortunately, he erred when he maintained, "The Constitution of the United States was ordained and established not by the States in their sovereign capacities, but emphatically, as the preamble of the Constitution declares, by 'the people of the United States.'" That error was the basis for his flawed reasoning leading to the conclusion that the appellate power of the Supreme Court extended to the State courts.

In Hylton v. United States, the Court had declared that the Constitution was an "accommodating system", which it is not. In Marbury v. Madison, the Court had asserted that, "It is emphatically the duty of the Judicial Department to say what the law is.", which it is not. In Fletcher v. Peck, the Court assumed the power to void State laws, which the Constitution does not permit. In Martin v. Hunter's Lessee, the court assumed the power to supervise State courts, a power the Court even admitted it was not granted.

But the greatest and most dangerous blunder in this case was the assertion by the Court that the States had not established the Constitution. The goal of the Redcoat is to destroy the political power of the States so that only the power of the central government remains.

In fact, the States were the only ones who created the Constitution. States sent delegates to the Philadelphia Convention and those delegates voted as States. States created ratifying conventions in which the Constitution was adopted. States recorded and certified ratifications. State representatives in Congress reported ratifications. Clearly, expressly, unequivocally, State legislatures created the federal government to serve them.

Clearly, expressly, unequivocally, "the people" had nothing to do with the creation and establishment of the Constitution. They did not vote for delegates, they did not vote to ratify. The Constitution was created by the States in the name of "the people" because the authority to act had been derived through representatives of "the people". The King of Spain did not set foot on America and claim the land, Columbus stood on American soil and claimed it in the name of the King.

John Marshall did not light the fire of the nationalist judiciary, but none more than he fanned the flames. Unfortunately, in 1816, he was just getting started.

In 1819, in the case of McCulloch v. Maryland, Marshall unleashed his greatest attack against the federal republic of America. His less than cogent opinion has been deemed to have declared that Article I, Section 8 of the Constitution, the Necessary And Proper Clause, confers "implied powers" on Congress so that Congress is not limited to its enumerated powers. Marshall wrote, "Let the ends be legitimate, let it be within the scope of the Constitution, and all means which are appropriate, which are plainly adopted to that end, which are not prohibited, but consist with the letter and spirit of the Constitution, are constitutional."

Marshall held that the sovereignty of the Union lay, not with the States which had won their sovereignty through war with England, but with the people of the United States. Because the 10th Amendment did not contain the word "expressly", because it "declares only" about powers, Marshall concluded the amendment cannot be construed as limiting Congressional power, and actually leaves the door open for more Congressional power.

James Madison said of the McCulloch decision that if the people of Virginia had known that the Constitution would be interpreted as giving Congress broad, discretionary powers, they would not have ratified the Constitution. Jefferson was more effusive in disparaging the Supreme Court's decision in McCulloch. He declared in 1820, "The judiciary of the United States is the subtle corps of sappers and miners constantly working under ground to undermine the foundations of our confederated republic. They are construing our constitution from a co-ordination of a general and special government to a general and supreme one alone."

As early as 1820, Thomas Jefferson, author of the Declaration of Independence and one of our republic's founders, could see that nationalist forces in the country, using usurpation as a tactic, were destroying the federal government he had helped to formulate. All the while, the legislatures in the States had the power to restrain the Congress, the Supreme Court, and the President. But they did not and the Redcoat agenda moved on through the other branches of the federal government.

USURPATION TWO
ABRAHAM LINCOLN: CREATION OF THE NATIONALIST UNION

President Abraham Lincoln did not preserve the federal Union. He destroyed the American federal republic by force, by law and by spirit. Fortunately, the concept and the history of the federal republic in America survived the scourge of Lincoln.

Lincoln began his breach of the Constitution shortly after his inauguration when he declared a blockade of southern ports on April 19, 1861. The President has no constitutional power to declare a blockade. That power belongs to the Congress. Lincoln deliberately and knowingly usurped legislative power expressly forbidden to the Executive branch of government. His blockade proclamation needlessly cites the law of nations because the law of nations only permitted blockades of warring countries. Dishonest Abe did not cite a foreign country as the object of the blockade and he took the trouble to identify the targeted States by name, as King George III had done when he acknowledged the freedom and sovereignty of those very same States in the Treaty Of Paris of 1783.

Lincoln next breached the Constitution when, in 1861, he suspended the writ of habeas corpus and empowered his generals to do the same. The Constitution is crystal clear that only Congress has the power to suspend habeas corpus. Once again, Dishonest Abe usurped legislative power expressly forbidden to the Executive branch. With habeas corpus illegally and summarily suspended, Dishonest Abe proceeded to detain, arrest, imprison and punish critics of his war policy.

In so doing, Lincoln usurped the power of the judiciary. In imprisoning and punishing people without lawful trial, Dishonest Abe was executing Bills of Attainder, which were clearly, expressly, decisively, unambiguously prohibited by the Constitution of the United States.

In 1861, in the case Ex parte Merryman, the Supreme Court under Chief Justice Taney ruled that Lincoln's 1861 suspension of habeas corpus was unconstitutional. Dishonest Abe had already forever disgraced himself as the Constitution-Violator-In-Chief. But he wasn't done yet.

On September 24, 1862, Lincoln suspended habeas corpus again. Even though the Supreme Court had already ruled this action illegal, Lincoln, the Illinois lawyer, did it again. Again, he illegally stifled dissent. When legislation in 1863 required that he provide lists of those he had illegally imprisoned, Lincoln simply ignored it.

On January 1, 1863, Lincoln issued the Emancipation Proclamation. In claiming the power to do this, Lincoln did not just violate the Constitution by again usurping legislative and judicial power, he was assuming the extra-constitutional power of tyranny by purporting to overrule State laws.

Lincoln did not accept the legality of the secession of the Confederate States, even though the Declaration Of Independence he admired was the colonial secession from Great Britain. However, in his last major trampling of the Constitution, he accepted the secession of West Virginia from Virginia by acknowledging statehood for the rebellious region on June 20, 1863.

By assuming all of the powers of government, in blatant violation of the Constitution, Lincoln destroyed the federal presidency and turned the office into a nationalist executive. Invasion of the South physically destroyed State governments while suspensions of habeas corpus, the blockade, and the Emancipation Proclamation politically destroyed State governments.

In addition to physically and operationally destroying State governments, the image of Union troops subduing States broke the spirit of the federal union. Without politically powerful States, there can be no federal union, only a nationalist tyranny. The States have not asserted their power since Lincoln and because of Lincoln. Memories of the vanquished and smoldering Confederacy stay the will of the States to emancipate themselves from their master, even in the North and the West.

The Confederate States seceded because the government in Washington, DC was not observing the Constitution. The New England States, who had threatened to secede during the Philadelphia Convention, were using the Congress to punish the South because the Kings of New England were not willing to abide by the Constitution's provisions regarding slavery.

The Confederate States were vanquished by a Union President who did not respect the federal Constitution that created his office. The quelling of the Confederate States of America was the largest defeat of federalism in American history. After Lincoln, the federal Union was no more. A nationalist union is all that remained. True power was vested in the nationalist government. The States were merely administrative units to carry out the programs of the exponentially expanding rogue Redcoat government.

General Robert E. Lee did not surrender only the Army of Northern Virginia, he relinquished the reality of federal States who possessed significant political power. Appomattox saw the end of States as deliberate, consenting bodies politic who protected the basic rights of their citizens—as they had since colonial times.

Lincoln abolished the government of the federal Union and imposed a rogue government of nationalist union. In the wake of the establishment of a nationalist judiciary and the military destruction of the federal union, the illegal, unconstitutional rogue Redcoat government grew unimpeded.

USURPATION THREE
WOODROW WILSON:
CREATION OF THE NATIONALIST EXECUTIVE

"The President is at liberty, both in law and in conscience, to be as big a man as he can."

Woodrow Wilson, 1908

Woodrow Wilson, a graduate of the College of New Jersey, was an academic political scientist who wrote extensively and passionately about the flaws of American constitutional government and also of his love for power. Long before he took office, Wilson's study of American government had revealed to him two constitutional loopholes in the restraint of executive power: foreign policy and governance by regulation.

Although a President could not declare war, a President could conduct foreign policy such that the threat of conflict would encourage Congress to allow him more leeway. If his foreign policy did lead to war, a President could use that emergency to greatly increase his regulatory administration, thus increasing his power.

Even if peace eventually removed most of the President's new regulatory apparatus, it might leave much of it in place. Regulatory precedent would also make it easier to get new laws passed that extended the reach of the government. An unabashed Calvinist, Thomas Woodrow Wilson loved his God; but as his works revealed, he loved power even more.

Wilson was elected President in 1912 and took office on March 4, 1913. In April of 1914 he got his chance to execute foreign policy without constraint by Congress. A Mexican general named Huerta had toppled the government of Mexico in a coup. Wilson did not support Huerta. When a few sailors were accidentally detained in Tampico, Wilson asked Congress for permission to use military force. When the House approved and the Senate declined, Wilson still sent the U.S. Marines into the port city of Vera Cruz. The occupation lasted a few months and Huerta fled the Mexican capital.

When turmoil in Haiti threatened U.S. interests in 1915, Wilson sent U.S. Marines to invade the country in July 1915. Wilson had no authority from Congress to invade Haiti and the occupation of that country continued until 1934.

In May of 1916, again without approval from Congress, Wilson invaded the Dominican Republic. Also in 1916, on his own authority, Wilson sent U.S. troops into Mexico in a futile attempt to capture Pancho Villa.

In 1917, the House voted to arm U.S. merchant ships in response to repeated sinking by German submarines. The Senate was locked in a filibuster and did not give its approval before Wilson issued an executive order in March to arm merchant vessels of the United States. Once again, Wilson usurped legislative power.

Concerned about the Bolshevik revolution in Russia, Wilson sent U.S. troops to Siberia in 1918. He did so, of course, on his own authority.

As he had deduced even before he took office, Wilson had greatly expanded his executive power through military adventures. The entry of America into World War I in 1917 gave Wilson the occasion to implement his second avenue of executive power expansion on a massive scale: government regulatory agencies and regulations.

On July 28, 1917, the War Industries Board was created by Wilson's Council Of National Defense. The ostensible purpose of the WIB was to guarantee that necessary raw materials and resources were available for war production. The true purpose of the WIB, and the scores of agencies, committees and boards that Wilson was to create, was to nationalize industry and socialize the population.

"Woe be to the man or group of men that seeks to stand in our way," Wilson declared in June 1917. WIB member and agency historian, Grosvenor Clarkson, described the WIB thusly, "It was an industrial dictatorship without parallel—a dictatorship by force of necessity and common consent which step by step at last encompassed the Nation and united it into a coordinated and mobile whole."

Of course, far from common consent, the WIB was created solely by a nationalist executive in the White House, a man who had scorned the U.S. Constitution for most of his academic career.

Wilson sought to nationalize thought when, prior to Lenin, Mussolini and Hitler, he established a government propaganda ministry when he created the Committee on Public Information. The CPI created and distributed millions of posters, pamphlets, press releases, and buttons and many propaganda films. At its height, the CPI had twenty subdivisions throughout America and the world.

To assist the CPI in the nationalization of thought, Wilson's Justice Department established the American Protective League to nationalize citizen behavior. The purpose of the APL was to spy on citizens by tapping their phones, reading their mail, and surveilling their activities. The APL grew to have a membership of a quarter of a million people and offices in six hundred cities and towns.

Unfortunately, the end of World War I did not mean the total dismantling of the nationalist expansion of executive power achieved through war powers and via nationalist agencies and regulations. The residue of Wilson's anti-federal hubris was the groundwork for the next great Redcoat assault led by Franklin Delano Roosevelt.

USURPATION FOUR
FRANKLIN DELANO ROOSEVELT: CREATION OF THE NATIONALIST LEGISLATURE

"...what we were doing in this country were some of the things that were being done in Russia and even some of the things that were being done under Hitler in Germany. But we were doing them in an orderly way."

FDR's confession to Harold Ickes, Interior Secretary and major architect of the New Deal

The stock market crash of October 24, 1929, was presaged by a sharp recession in the spring of 1928. The smart money got out of the market with their profits while stock prices—and unemployment—soared. At the same time, Americans were engaged in a credit craze, buying homes, cars, jewels, college educations, and stock with credit. Before the credit bubble popped, three hundred million shares were held on margin. As the Depression worsened, commodity prices fell sharply and banks began to fail. Just before FDR took office on March 4, 1933, a run on the banks caused depositors to lose thirty billion dollars.

Before the Depression, American citizens viewed the role of the federal government as secondary to the role of their State governments. The severe hardships unleashed by the Depression caused the public to appeal first to Congress and then, under Hoover, to the President to do something to fix their miserable condition. By the time FDR succeeded Hoover, the desperate citizenry was urgently, though not wisely, prepared to cede powers formerly exercised by the States to the Congress and to the Executive branch. The stage was set for Wilson's fascist "administrative state" to be constituted within the purview of the President.

FDR eagerly implemented this administrative oligarchy which rendered the Congress a mere clerical branch of government. The federal Congress was composed of representatives of the States who deliberated and enacted legislation that promoted the interests of the States while simultaneously protecting the States from encroachment by the central government. Using the Depression as Wilson had used World War I to implement massive social engineering, FDR transformed the Congress into a nationalist legislature. Democratic majorities in both houses made it easy for FDR to fashion a Congress that no longer addressed the needs of the States who had created that Congress.

The New Deal that FDR imposed on America was simply this: the old-deal federal Congress would cease to function and a new-deal nationalist Congress would take its place. This Redcoat Congress, which would have received Alexander Hamilton's blessing, did not view the Republic as a federation of powerful States, but as one nation. States and their constitutional, as well as traditional powers, were dismissed. Congress acted as if it had a constituency of one, the one specifically prohibited by the Constitution: "the people."

Five days after being inaugurated, FDR called Congress into a special session. The effort to combat the terrible Depression had been presented to the public as essentially a war effort. Congress was eager to do FDR's bidding with legislation and to accord him great leeway, as if giving him war powers, when he ignored Congress or defied Congress and the Supreme Court. This special session of Congress marked the beginning of what would come to be called "the Hundred Days."

FDR immediately gave Congress the Emergency Banking Act of 1933 and they passed it on March 19, 1933, adding legislation to create the FDIC. FDR then had the power to regulate the banking system and he declared a banking holiday. Constitutionally, only Congress and the States could regulate banks. The nationalist Congress, which did not recognize the separation of powers nor the existence of States, conferred the power to regulate banks on the President. The very next day, March 20, 1933, continuing its unconstitutional Redcoat agenda, Congress passed the Economy Act of 1933, giving FDR the power to control the pensions of veterans and the salaries of federal government employees.

Congress next passed, in May, the Agricultural Adjustment Act of 1933 that gave Roosevelt the power to control agricultural commodity prices and, via the Thomas Amendment, to control the currency. Again, the Redcoat Congress overlooked the existence of States and the separation of powers. The seminal piece of the nationalist New Deal came on June 16, 1933 with the passage of the National Industrial Recovery Act of 1933, which basically gave FDR the power to organize, regulate and control the entire industrial sector of the American economy.

Congress and the Executive branch continue to function in the framework of the New Deal. That framework is simply this: Congress and the Executive Branch will continue to trivialize the States as long as the States allow them to do so. The New Deal was a constitutional Raw Deal and its legacy must be stopped dead in its tracks.

USURPATION FIVE
THE FEDERAL RESERVE: CREATION OF THE NATIONALIST ECONOMY

"The central bank is an institution of the most deadly hostility existing against the Principles and form of our Constitution. I am an Enemy to all banks discounting bills or notes for anything but Coin. If the American People allow private banks to control the issuance of their currency, first by inflation and then by deflation, the banks and corporations that will grow up around them will deprive the People of all their Property until their Children will wake up homeless on the continent their Fathers conquered."

Thomas Jefferson

"We have in this country one of the most corrupt institutions the world has ever known. I refer to the Federal Reserve Board and the Federal Reserve Banks. Some people think the Federal Reserve Banks are U.S. government institutions. They are not government institutions. They are private credit monopolies; domestic swindlers, rich and predatory money lenders which prey upon the people of the United States for the benefit of themselves and their foreign customers. The Federal Reserve Banks are the agents of the foreign central banks. The truth is the Federal Reserve Board has usurped the Government of the United States by the arrogant credit monopoly which operates the Federal Reserve Board."

Congressman Louis T. McFadden, Chairman of the House Banking & Currency Committee, speech on the floor of the House of Representatives, June 10, 1932

From colonial times until 1913, America operated with a real economy in which commercial activity was predominantly the result of individual enterprise with a medium of exchange that was tangible and the role of government was to keep currency in an adequate supply. After 1776, thirteen State economies functioned independently and this method was sufficient to allow the country to grow and to expand by adding additional independent State economies. Only in times of war was anyone concerned about the country's economy being able to provide the armaments and supplies for victory.

Therefore, it was in times of war that the central government increased its grip on the economies of the States. The economic uncertainty, bank failures and depression following the Spanish American War in 1898 provided the right environment for the central government to make a grab for greater control of the economic activity of the States. The passage of the Aldrich-Vreeland Act of 1908 created the National Monetary Commission, which was charged with finding a structural solution to the problems of liquidity and bank panics.

This simple action contained the assumption that America possessed a nationalist economy, which it did not and could not since it was neither a nation nor governed by a single authority. This error of conception would lead to the destruction of the real economies in America and their replacement by a totally fictitious nationalist economy completely controlled by the central government. The work of the National Monetary Commission led to various proposals which culminated in the Federal Reserve Act of 1913 being signed into law by President Wilson on December 23, 1913. Ensuing legislation gave the Federal Reserve, a private corporation, more and more power: the Banking Act of 1935, the Bank Holding Company Act of 1956, the International Banking Act of 1978, the Federal Deposit Insurance Corporation Improvement Act of 1991, the Gramm-Leach-Bliley Act of 1999, and the Emergency Economic Stabilization Act of 2008.

The reason that the Congress has gleefully given more power to the Federal Reserve, even though the Congress cannot audit the books of the Federal Reserve to see where the money is really going, is that the Congress—unlike the public—knows why the Federal Reserve was actually created. The Federal Reserve was created in secret sessions because the public would not tolerate the truth.

The Federal Reserve was not created to solve banking and liquidity problems; in fact, it can't and has precipitated several banking and liquidity crises since its surreptitious inception. The Federal Reserve was created to establish a phony economy that would be completely controlled by the central government and that would provide for the exponential increase in the size and power of the central government regardless of economic conditions.

Before 1913, real economies existed in the States and tax receipts of real money and the sale of government bonds for real money financed the operations of government. Congressional appropriations caused real money to change hands, the United States Treasury held real money and there was real gold in Fort Knox. United States and foreign banking cartels devised the Federal Reserve system so that private banks would control the central banking functions of an economy that would be structured to be nationalist, would not rely on real money, and would fund the government without limitation.

This shady scheme to nationalize the economy required two components: a banking system and government accounting system that did not require real money and, secondly, a fiat currency, a currency backed only by the credit of the US government. Several years were required for the Federal Reserve to generate the phony economy but the establishment of a fiat currency took even longer. People were accustomed to money having real value but, under the pretext of controlling runs on banks,

FDR and the Congress nationalized gold and dispossessed the population. In 1971 President Nixon and Congress removed the U.S. from the gold standard.

From that historic moment in 1971, when the last shred of the real economy disappeared from America, economic activity in the United States has been completely controlled by the central government using the nationalistic model of the sovereign sole currency issuer.

Under this model, only the sovereign central government may issue currency; the government may issue an unlimited amount of currency; the central government can never run out of money; taxes are not used to fund the government but to drain excess currency from circulation; government accounts are based on credits that do not represent actual currency; actual currency is not maintained in the Treasury; banks within the Federal Reserve system do not exchange actual currency; the sale of government bonds does not fund the central government but merely controls the inter-banking interest rate; deficits are of no concern because the government can issue as much currency as it likes; there is no actual currency or gold in Fort Knox; the Federal Reserve buys massive amounts of government debt and charges the taxpayers a fee for maintaining the ruse that the bonds finance the government; and no one is supposed to admit that private banks make a fortune from this scheme and the government is unimpeded in its expansion and its ability to make war.

The nationalist economy operating in the United States today functions exactly as the model just described. The President, the Congress, the Supreme Court, the Republican politicians, and the Democrat politicians know that this phony economy controls America. Each has done its part to put this scheme in place so that the power of the central government can be endlessly expanded and the dependence of the people on the central government can be extended without limit.

Only the States can destroy this Redcoat scourge and restore the real, independent economies of the States.

THE CONSTITUTIONAL IMPERATIVE

Authority is superior to law because law is derived from authority. Our history is a bloody testament to this truth. The Constitution is the highest expression of principle in the United States, but the Constitution is inferior to the bodies politic that created it: the legislatures of the States. As such, the Constitution is not the final arbiter of law in the United States and neither is the Supreme Court: that power lies with the legislatures of the States and they have shamelessly refused to assert that prerogative and have allowed our government to decay from a bicameral federation of States into the one form of government that the Constitution specifically prohibits: a nationalist government.

Our current rogue Redcoat government is patently unconstitutional and must be brought down now, not by force of arms, but by the legislatures of the States executing the force of individual amendment. The Palmetto Manifesto presented in this book is a plan of attack for the State legislatures to demolish the imperial Redcoat government in Washington, DC.

The Manifesto attacks the nationalist government on seven major fronts: the restraint of federal political power with Articles 1, 2, 4, 6, 7, 8, 9, 15, 17, 21, 22, 24; restraint of federal taxing power with Articles 3, 5; restraint of federal war power with

Articles 10, 25; restraint of federal political careers with Articles 11, 12, 13, 14; restraint of federal citizenship power with Articles 16, 18, 19; restraint of federal economic power with Article 20; and restraint of federal cultural power with Article 23.

If the States enact the articles of the Manifesto as amendments to the Constitution, their State Rebellion will restore our federal union, restore our federal legislature, restore our federal judiciary, and restore our real economy. True economic forces, operating independently in the States, with a real currency of stable value will allow the States to maintain a short leash on the federal dogs that must do the bidding of the States that created them. If the States fail to act, the Republic will perish and the light of the world will succumb to barbarian darkness and unspeakable evil.

Rise up, States! Rebel! Time is short and the States—without which there can be no federal Republic—are drowning in the Redcoat tide spewing out of Washington, DC.

THE PALMETTO MANIFESTO

To rein in the rogue nationalist government, the Palmetto Manifesto should be enacted as a series of amendments which the States should pass in Congress and send to the States for ratification. May the State of South Carolina take the lead in adopting the Palmetto Manifesto!

South Carolina patriots, in the battle of Cowpens, provided the seminal victory that won the Revolutionary War against the illegitimate government of the king of England. South Carolina federalists, by voting to secede in Charleston, provided the seminal act of defiance against the illegitimate government of the kings of New England. Let it then be South Carolina that provides the seminal amendment from the Palmetto Manifesto which will bring down the illegitimate government of the Redcoats now occupying Washington, DC.

Should the States fail to act soon, there will be a second shot heard round the world but it will not portend the arrival of greater liberty. That dreaded sound will proclaim the end of the American quest for liberty as the last constitutional federalist is shot dead by agents of the Redcoat government.

The constitutional federal patriots of South Carolina and the other States of the federal union demand that the Articles of this Palmetto Manifesto be added as amendments to the Constitution forthwith.

Summary of The Palmetto Manifesto

Article One: Federal Government Power Restricted To Enumerated Powers

Article Two: A Super-Majority Of State Legislatures Can Overturn Any Federal Act

Article Three: Power To Tax Withdrawn From Federal Government And Given To State Governments

Article Four: Withdraw The Popular Election Of Senators And Return The Power To Appoint Senators To State Legislatures

Article Five: Abolish The Income Tax, The IRS, And The US Tax Code

Article Six: Presidents Must First Serve As Governor

Article Seven: Senators Must First Serve As Mayor

Article Eight: House Members Must First Serve As County Commissioner

Article Nine: Supreme Court Justices Must First Serve As Magistrate

Article Ten: War Powers Abolished And The Power To Declare War Returned To The States

Article Eleven: Senators And House Members Serve One Term

Article Twelve: Congress Members May Serve Either In The Senate Or The House But Not Both

Article Thirteen: Members Of Congress May Not Serve In Cabinet

Article Fourteen: Cabinet Members May Not Serve In House Or Senate

Article Fifteen: Ambassadors Must First Serve As Secretary Of State For One Of The States

Article Sixteen: Presidents Must Be Born In One Of The States

Article Seventeen: Treaties Are Inferior To US Law

Article Eighteen: Birth Citizenship Restricted To Children Of US Citizens

Article Nineteen: Legal Entry Required For Immigrant Citizenship

Article Twenty: Abolition Of The Federal Reserve And Return To The Gold Standard

Article Twenty-One: Hate Speech Protected And Hate Crimes Abolished

Article Twenty-Two: US Membership In United Nations Withdrawn And Membership In Global Governance Organizations Forbidden

Article Twenty-Three: Abolition Of US Dept. Of Education; Master's Degree Required To Teach; Schools Must Be Funded By General Fund Of State

Article Twenty-Four: Commerce Clause Restricted To Actual Commerce

Article Twenty-Five: Volunteer Military Service Abolished; Universal Conscription Established; Military Service Restricted To Military Approved Combatants

ARTICLE 1: Federal Power Permanently Restrained

FEDERAL POWER PERMANENTLY RESTRAINED: THE CONSTITUTION AND THE STATES ARE THE FINAL ARBITERS OF THE POWERS OF THE FEDERAL GOVERNMENT, FEDERAL GOVERNMENT FORBIDDEN FROM ASSUMING POWERS NOT ENUMERATED IN CONSTITUTION

"This Constitution is a compact only among the sovereign States that ratify it; the government of the United States created by this Constitution is not a party to this compact; the peoples of the States are not parties to this compact. The legislatures of the ratifying States are the only parties to this compact and are the highest and final arbiter of the powers of the government of the United States herein created. Neither Congress, nor the government of the United States, nor the peoples of the States shall be superior to the legislatures of the ratifying States in determining, and providing a remedy, when the government of the United States exceeds its expressly enumerated powers, the only powers granted to it by this Constitution and the only powers it may lawfully possess, exercise, and from which it may receive benefit."

Need For Article 1

"Liberty, the greatest of all earthly blessings—give us that precious jewel, and you may take everything else!....Guard with jealous attention the public liberty, suspect everyone who approaches that jewel."

Patrick Henry, June 5, 1788

The rogue nationalist government in Washington, DC has assumed and exercised vast powers not granted to it by the Constitution. The fear that the central government would exceed its delegated powers was the major concern of the Framers as they debated the structure of the government they were creating. The restraint they designed to contain the new central government was the appointment of Senators by State legislatures. The Senators, being thus appointed and serving at pleasure of the State legislatures, would represent the interests of the State legislatures—not the people in the States—and protect the States from the central government.

Since the State legislatures were creating the central government, they needed their own watchdogs over the new government. Senators would be those guardians—as long as they were appointed by the State legislatures. The 17th amendment, ratified in 1913, removed Senators as representatives for the State legislatures by having them elected by the people in the States.

This ill-conceived amendment destroyed our bicameral Congress and gave us a single chamber of nationalist legislation responsible only to the people. Although we have two houses of Congress in name, in function and power, we only have one. Only the people in the States have representation in the central government. The 17th amendment began the destruction of our federal government because it abolished the authority of the State legislatures in the central government. The former federation of State legislatures, that had made the central government federal in nature and limited by State authority, disappeared. America now had a functioning nationalist government, even though the Constitution prohibited this type of government by defining two distinct levels of power: the central government and the State governments.

The States still existed in name, and in reality at the State level of government, but the 17th amendment erased the States as checks against the central government. Unchecked, the nationalist government has seized powers not granted to it, by its own arrogance and by the arrogance of its Special Forces, the Justices of the Supreme Court. The Supreme Court has rapaciously extended its own power, and thus that of the central government. Conspicuously ignoring the 10th Amendment, the Court has used the Commerce Clause, the Necessary and Proper Clause, the 14th Amendment and specious reasoning to radically expand the power of the central government beyond the powers given to it in the Constitution.

Article 1, ratified as an amendment, is needed to establish the State legislatures as the masters of the central government they created to serve them; to limit the central government to just those powers expressly given to it by the Constitution; to establish that the State legislatures are the final arbiters of the powers of the central government, not the Supreme Court; and to make it crystal clear that both the central government and the people in the States are not parties to the Constitution and that popular will can never be superior in authority to the will of the State legislatures expressed through the Constitution.

Effect of Article 1

Ratification of an Amendment enacting Article 1 would immediately bar the Supreme Court from conferring to the central government powers that are not expressly delegated by the Constitution. In addition, this amendment would provide the basis for lawsuits to force the Supreme Court to reverse earlier decisions which had attributed powers to the central government that are not expressly delegated in the Constitution.

Supreme Court rulings regarding the separation of church and state, the use of the Commerce Clause to extend the power of the central government, enforcing the Bill of Rights against the States, abortion, and affirmative action, when challenged, would have to be brought in line with the Constitution. The supremacy of the State legislatures would be established in theory, law and fact.

ARTICLE 2: Super-majority Of States May Renounce Any Federal Action

STATES TO RESTRAIN ACTIONS OF U.S. SUPREME COURT, U.S. CONGRESS, U.S. PRESIDENT, AND U.S. TREATIES

"Any law, treaty or treaty provision, declaration of war, Supreme Court decision or order, or Presidential executive order shall be repealed, revoked, rescinded, vacated and shall be null and void when three-quarters of the legislatures of the States have lawfully adopted a Resolution of Renunciation particularly identifying and renouncing that law, treaty or treaty provision, declaration of war, Supreme Court decision or order, or Presidential executive order."

Need For Article 2

"On every question of construction let us carry ourselves back to the time when the Constitution was adopted, recollect the spirit manifested in the debates, and instead of trying what meaning can be squeezed out of the text, or invented against it, conform to the probable one which was passed."

Thomas Jefferson

The Articles Of Confederation, ratified March 1, 1781 created the first federal government in America. The Constitution, ratified by New Hampshire on June 21, 1788, became effective and expanded the power of the federal government. However, this expansion was consented to by the States and was strictly limited by the carefully chosen, ardently debated, text of the empowering document.

The newly created federal government did not delay in seeking to augment its powers beyond the strict, clear delineations the States had prescribed. In 1819, under Chief Justice John Marshall, in the case McCulloch v. Maryland, the Supreme Court ruled that Congress was not limited to the powers explicitly given to it by the Constitution. The Court held that Article I, Section 8, the Necessary and Proper Clause, conferred on the Congress broad "implied powers" to implement its enumerated powers.

The carefully designed system of checks and balances for the federal government, just ratified in 1788, was broken by this ill-conceived ruling. Marshall could not have been ignorant of the fact that the States feared unchecked federal power more than anything else when they had crafted a government with strictly enumerated powers. Marshall desired to increase the prestige of the Court, to establish that it had equal rank with the executive and legislative branches. This case gave him that opportunity and he took it, heedless of the consequences of his rashness and in dereliction of his duty to adhere to express delegation of power in the Constitution.

In addition to creating unchecked power for Congress, the Court in this case also declared sovereignty rested with the people of the United States, not with the States. Evidently, Chief Justice Marshall was unfamiliar with the Treaty of Paris of 1783, the Articles of Confederation, and the Mayflower Compact. Sovereignty is not about power, sovereignty is about authority. The Court was perfectly aware that the people of the United States are not parties to the Constitution, that the central government of which the Court was a part, had been created by the State legislatures to SERVE the State legislatures.

In McCulloch v. Maryland, the Court disgraced itself by flouting the very document and principles that had brought it into existence. The Court humiliated itself but it increased its own power; to do so, the Court had to invent "implied powers" that left the powers of Congress completely unchecked. The crucial point is that the Court put its ambition ahead of its duty and nothing in the Constitution could prevent its action.

The 17th Amendment removed the Senate as the power of the States to check the ambitions of the central government; the predilection of the Supreme Court to enhance its own prestige has removed the Court as a check against the ambitions of the Congress and the Executive branch of the central government. The States, who have been abjectly derelict in their duty to regulate the central government they created must have the effective means to restrain and direct the central government. Article 2, ratified as an Amendment, would provide such means.

Effect of Article 2

Ratification of an Amendment enacting this Article would allow the States to immediately challenge any law, treaty or treaty provision, declaration of war, Supreme Court decision or order, and Presidential executive order by passing a Resolution Of Renunciation and attempting to get ¾ of the States to adopt the same Resolution. The States would have the power to completely control the actions of the central government. A three-fourths majority would be difficult to achieve so only the most offensive acts of the central government would be reversed but, going forward, the central government would give more heed to the desires of the States which it serves.

ARTICLE 3: States To Collect Federal Tax Defined In Constitution

WITHDRAW THE POWER TO TAX FROM THE FEDERAL GOVERNMENT AND RETURN THAT POWER TO THE STATES; ESTABLISH A SINGLE FEDERAL TAX AND TAX RATE TO BE COLLECTED AND ADMINISTERED BY THE STATES; PAY THE OPERATING COSTS OF THE FEDERAL GOVERNMENT ONLY UPON COMPLETION OF A COMPREHENSIVE YEARLY BUDGET

"Section 1: The government of the United States of America shall not have the power to levy or impose taxes. The government of the United States of America shall receive from the States, once yearly, operating funds equal to the amount of monies specified in the lawfully adopted complete budget for the United States government created by Congress for that particular year. Continuing resolutions shall not constitute adoption of a complete budget. If Congress fails to lawfully adopt a complete budget for a particular year, no funds of any kind shall be provided to the government of the United States by the States.

Section 2: The States shall have the power to levy, impose and collect a single federal tax on a single federal tax entity at a single rate not to exceed four percent of the value of the federal tax entity. The sole federal tax entity shall consist of a distinct transaction of commerce which requires the jurisdiction of the State courts for its legal existence, enforcement, valuation, dispute resolution, or damage consideration. All revenue generated by the federal tax entity and collected by the States and not paid to the government of the United States to fund its yearly operating budget shall be retained by the States and shall become the property of the States.

Section 3: In making payment to the government of the United States of tax revenue collected via the federal tax for the amount of monies specified in the lawfully adopted, complete budget of a particular year, each State shall pay an amount equal to the percentage of the total federal budget for that year that is the same percentage of the total Representatives that State is entitled to have in the House of Representatives for that year.

Section 4: The District of Columbia is not a State, shall not become a State, and shall be directly and exclusively governed by the Congress of the United States."

Need For Article 3

"I wish it were possible to obtain a single amendment to our constitution. I would be willing to depend on that alone for the reduction of the administration of our government to the general principles of its constitution; I mean an additional article, taking from our federal government the power of borrowing."

Thomas Jefferson, November 26, 1798

Although borrowing is not the same as taxing, it does make funds available to the government. Restricting the central government purse was a major concern of the Framers and has been ardently advised by several U.S. presidents. Every president has nonetheless found his own reasons for aligning with the Congress to expand the federal budget. Each expansion increases the size and power of government, depletes the public funds and results in a request for more federal spending. The people have done nothing to end this cancer and the States have stood idly by while the Republic pompously marches headlong toward ruin.

The central government has greatly abused its power to tax and has proven that it will never effectively reduce the great burden of taxes it has imposed on the people. With few exceptions, the central government has not effected remedies for the distress of the people. Rather, it has singularly used its power to tax simply to increase its own power and expand its bureaucratic intrusion into the liberties of the people. The duty to pay for the central government belongs to the States who created it; the power to tax to support that central government therefore belongs to the States.

Because this Article transfers great power back to the States, it is necessary to specify that the District of Columbia is not a State and shall not become a State.

Effect Of Article 3

Ratification of an Amendment enacting this Article would remove the power of the federal government to tax or to receive or manipulate tax revenue. This single change in how the federal government is funded would accomplish the fundamental basis for returning the central government to a true federal government. Our constitutional federal government was created to serve, not the people of the States but the governments of the States, which in turn serve their people. In other words, the federal government works for the States, not the citizens of the States. Allowing only the States to collect the operating funds for the federal government makes it clear that the federal government serves the governments of the States.

Ratification of the enacting Amendment would immediately give the federal government a vested interest in the real economic growth of the States. Since the only entity for the federal tax is commercial transactions and the tax rate cannot exceed four percent, the federal government would want more transactions with higher economic value so it could appeal to the States for more funding. This enacting amendment would put an immediate end to the economic treason the government in Washington, DC has been committing against the people of the United States for the last 100 years.

Government policy, implemented by both political parties, deliberately destroyed our manufacturing base and forced us into an inferior, low-wage, debt-ridden service economy. Had this enacting amendment been in effect, the government in Washington, DC could not have given away the wealth of US economy to borrow the money to fund expensive programs and entitlements to keep career political leaders in power.

Ratification of this Amendment would ensure that a lawful budget is adopted on time each year. "Continuing resolutions" would not constitute adoption of a yearly budget so the federal government would not receive its operating funds from the States. Congress would be forced to complete a budget every year.

A single federal tax not to exceed 4% would be applied to commercial transactions executed in the States, territories or possessions. This federal tax would be collected and held by the States until an operating budget for the federal government was lawfully adopted by the States in Congress. The budgeted amount would then be paid by the States into the federal Treasury. Each State would pay a portion of the budget that is equal to the ratio of that State's Representatives to all the members of the House of Representatives.

Because the federal tax entity and the federal tax rate are set in the Constitution, Congress would be unable to raise taxes except by amending the

Constitution and having the States ratify the new amendment.

ARTICLE 4: Senators Appointed By State Legislatures

RESTORE THE PURPOSE OF THE BICAMERAL CONGRESS CREATED IN THE CONSTITUTION WHEREIN THE SENATE WAS TO PROTECT THE STATES FROM THE FEDERAL GOVERNMENT AND THE HOUSE WAS TO PROTECT THE PEOPLE IN THE STATES FROM THE FEDERAL GOVERNMENT: WITHDRAW THE POPULAR ELECTION OF SENATORS AND RETURN THE POWER TO APPOINT SENATORS TO THE LEGISLATURES OF THE STATES

"The 17th amendment is hereby repealed."

Need For Article 4

"A little rebellion now and then is a good thing."

Thomas Jefferson

Because the States reluctantly created a central government and gave it limited powers, they wanted a method to watch this central government and make sure it stayed within the bounds they had given it. The Senate was the regulatory mechanism they chose. Senators were appointed by the State legislatures because their purpose was to represent the States in Congress and protect the States against the central government. The social conditions in the early 1900s led to two disastrous amendments in 1913: the 16th, allowing an income tax, and the 17th, destroying the bicameral congress and eliminating the representation of the States in Congress.

After 1913, only the people were represented in Congress. The people did not create the Constitution and the people are not parties to the Constitution, yet suddenly only they spoke in Congress. The entities which had created the Constitution, and the only parties to the Constitution, the States, were no longer represented in Congress and had no effective check against the central government. The unchecked central government has continued to grow and will completely efface the States until it is forcefully stopped by the States. This Article is a vital weapon for the States in the battle to constitutionally contain the central government.

Effect of Article 4

Ratification of an Amendment enacting this Article would immediately end the election of Senators by popular vote and return to the original method of having Senators appointed by State legislatures. The original purpose of Senators was to represent State governments in Congress. This was important because members of the House of

Representatives were elected by the people of the States to protect the people of the States from the federal government. Senators were originally appointed by State legislatures to protect State legislatures from the federal government.

When the 17th Amendment was ratified, one house of Congress was effectively lost. We had two houses, both popularly elected, and both serving to protect the people of the States from the federal government. However, there was then no house in Congress to protect State legislatures from the federal government and the federal government began to usurp the powers given to the States by the Constitution. Repealing the 17th Amendment restores the original structure, function, and balance of protection to the Congress.

ARTICLE 5: Abolition Of Income Tax

RESTRAIN THE FEDERAL PURSE:
ABOLISH THE INCOME TAX, THE IRS AND THE US TAX CODE

"The 16th Amendment is hereby repealed; all laws enacted by Congress to create, administer, collect, and disburse income tax revenue or any per capita tax are hereby repealed, abolished and declared null and void."

Need For Article 5

The central government has greatly abused its power to tax and has proven that it will never effectively reduce the great burden of taxes it has imposed on the people. With few exceptions, the central government has not effected remedies for the distress of the people. Rather, it has singularly used its power to tax simply to increase its own power and expand its bureaucratic intrusion into the liberties of the people.

Direct taxes were unconstitutional until 1913 when the 16th Amendment was ratified. The Framers knew that a direct tax by the central government was a serious threat to liberty so they prohibited such a tax. This Article simply restores a vital limitation on the central government that the Framers imposed for the greater protection of liberty.

Effect of Article 5

Ratification of an Amendment enacting this Article would abolish the income tax, the IRS and the entire US tax code. From the time the Constitution was adopted in 1789 until the 16th Amendment was ratified in 1913, the income tax was unconstitutional. The Framers were afraid of the power an income tax would give the new federal government to expand its powers, so they expressly forbade an income tax. Ratification of the amendment enacting this article would restore the original unconstitutionality of the income tax and abolish the IRS and the tax code. This amendment is needed to support the adoption of Article One and the creation of a single federal tax defined only in the Constitution. Congress would be unable to enact policy through a tax code and the per capita tax would once again be banned. This Article strips the central government of much of its power and its restraint on the central government is needed now, even more than it was when originally imposed in 1789.

ARTICLE 6: President Must First Be Governor

EXECUTIVE EXPERIENCE REQUIRED FOR U.S. PRESIDENT: PRESIDENT MUST FIRST SERVE AS GOVERNOR

"No person shall serve as President of the United States of America who has not previously been elected to and served one elected term in the office of Governor of one of the States."

Need For Article 6

The office of the President is the chief executive office in the land. Having someone in that office who has never had major executive experience in government is absurd and has led to disastrous results. Serving as a governor of one of the States as a prerequisite for serving as president will provide a reliable level of executive experience for the chief executive; ensure that the chief executive has some loyalty to the States; and prevent money and influence networks or popular hysteria from catapulting someone with no political executive experience into the White House.

Effect of Article 6

Ratification of an Amendment enacting this Article would immediately change presidential and State politics. The office of Governor would recover much of its former prestige because only State chief executives could become the President. Knowing that their governor could become President, the people in the States would require higher standards for gubernatorial candidates and a stricter code of conduct for governors in office.

State presidential primaries and the general election for president would be drastically altered because the public would have the documented gubernatorial record of anyone running for President. The executive experience of presidential candidates, when they were governors, would be open to scrutiny by anyone.

Ratification of this Article as an Amendment, would abolish the carefully calculated grip of political parties on the presidential election process. Best of all, the status of the States would be raised because they would become presidential nurseries.

ARTICLE 7: Senator Must First Be Mayor

ADVISORY EXPERIENCE REQUIRED FOR U.S. SENATOR: SENATOR MUST FIRST SERVE AS MAYOR

"No person shall serve as a Senator in the Senate of the United States of America who has not been previously been elected to and served an elected term in the office of mayor of an incorporated city in one of the States."

Need For Article 7

The original purpose of the Senate was to provide for direct representation of the State legislatures in the central government and to provide an advisory role to the President. Therefore, Senators were originally intended to have either advisory experience or experience that was broad enough to permit them to give advice. The foolhardiness of the 17th Amendment destroyed the purpose of the Senate and has made Senators nothing more than winners of popularity contests.

Domestic policy, foreign policy, and the health of the Republic have all suffered grievously because of the hysterical frenzy that resulted in the 16th and 17th Amendments in 1913. This Article is needed to help restore the health of the Republic by ensuring that Senators have first served as mayor, that they possess experience in giving advice, which mayors, whose powers are limited compared to their responsibilities, are required to give.

Ratification of this Article as an Amendment would also prevent political parties from stuffing the Senate with "good for the camera" candidates who can't advise their way out of a paper bag. Senatorial elections would be improved because the mayoral records of candidates would be documented and public.

Effect of Article 7

Ratification of an Amendment enacting this Article would ensure that Senators have advisory experience before assuming their high office. Senatorial elections would expose documented public records of advisory service as mayor. Media candidates could not run for the Senate unless they had previously served as mayor.

ARTICLE 8: House Member Must First Be County Commissioner

EXPERIENCE LEGISLATING SOLUTIONS TO THE IMMEDIATE PRACTICAL NEEDS OF THE PEOPLE REQUIRED FOR THE HOUSE: MEMBERS OF THE U.S. HOUSE OF REPRESENTATIVES MUST FIRST SERVE AS COUNTY COMMISSIONER

"No person shall serve as a Representative in the United States House of Representatives who has not been previously elected to and served an elected term in the office of county commissioner of a legally organized county of one of the States."

Need For Article 8

The purpose of the House of Representatives is to directly present the interests of the people in the States to the central government. This can best happen when the members of the House have prior experience actually legislating solutions to the urgent, pragmatic needs of the people. Service as a county commissioner would provide the needed experience and make House members more adept at translating practical need into effective legislation.

Effect of Article 8

Ratification of an Amendment enacting this Article would end the ability of political parties to fill the House of Representatives with media candidates who have no experience developing policies for pragmatic needs. House elections would improve because the records of the candidates as county commissioners would be documented and public.

ARTICLE 9: Supreme Court Justice Must First Be Magistrate

EXPERIENCE WITH THE DIRECT EFFECTS OF JUDICIAL DECISIONS REQUIRED FOR HIGHEST U.S. COURT: JUSTICES OF THE SUPREME COURT MUST FIRST SERVE AS MAGISTRATE

"No person shall serve as a Justice of the Supreme Court of the United States who has not served for at least three years as a Magistrate in one of the States."

Need For Article 9

The highest court in the land should have justices who have experience with the effects of their decisions. Historically, Supreme Court justices have been appointed because they have either curried favor with Presidents and their cronies, or because they have curried favor with the administrators and cronies of major law schools.

The result has been disastrous for the Republic because this cronyism has put either federal judges or legal scholars on the Supreme Court. While this might sound admirable, the problem is that federal judges and legal scholars have experience and allegiance to statutory and common law. Judgments at common law rely heavily on practices and precedent. Analysis of statutes involves the application of a statute to a set of facts. In the process, the intent of legislature can inform the meaning of the statute and the boundaries of the meaning of the statute are restricted by the constitution of the State involved.

The Constitution is neither statute law nor common law. The Constitution is an express compact binding those who ratified the agreement to the exact words that were ratified. The meaning of those words, at the time of ratification, is the meaning of the statements that were agreed to by the parties, the legislatures of the States. Agreeing to express statements that were understood by the ratifying parties was the entire purpose of the Constitution.

The intentions of the State legislatures, so important to statutory adjudication, are not a part of the Constitution because the purpose of the document was to remove this one compact from State and intra-State politics. In order to have the authority to compel the States to abide by its declarations, the Constitution had to clearly express what was being agreed to by the parties.

Precedent, crucial to all matters of common and statutory law, is also not in the Constitution. The purpose of the Constitution was to represent a new beginning for the interactions of the States. As such, it has no precedent because its charter was to have no precedent, to be an absolutely new beginning in which only the words within it, having the meaning they did when it was ratified, had any purpose or power.

Unfortunately, from its inception, the Supreme Court was ruled by an ambition to increase its prestige and by a statutory and common law approach to constitutional cases. Because the Court's approach was flawed at the outset, the Court felt free to, and still flagrantly does, ignore that the Constitution is an express compact whose meaning was fixed at ratification.

Magistrates understand that their words have fixed meanings, and immediate effects, when they say them. They should be disposed to understanding that the Constitution had fixed meaning when it was ratified.

Effect of Article 9

Ratification of an Amendment enacting this Article would immediately bar from appointment as Supreme Court justices those law school faculty who possess only academic careers. In addition, it would prohibit federal judges from serving on the high court if they had not served on the lowest court, the court closest to the people.

ARTICLE 10: War Powers Returned To States

MILITARY ADVENTURISM TERMINATED, WAR POWERS ABOLISHED: POWER TO DECLARE WAR RETURNED TO THE STATES

"Congress shall not have the power to declare war. The government of the United States of America shall not commence, execute, sustain, or commit any act of war, save necessary defense from attack, against the forces, governments, resources, or peoples of external enemies, unless and until a majority of the legislatures of the States, duly in session, have duly enacted and recorded a vote authorizing all necessary acts of war against a particular external enemy until the threat posed by that external enemy against the people of the United States has been eliminated."

Need For Article 10

"I flung forward the flag of the country, sure that the people would press onward and defend it."

James Madison in referring to the War of 1812

Since the end of World War II, America has been involved in the Vietnam war, the first Gulf war, the war in Iraq, and the war in Afghanistan yet Congress has failed to declare war. Citing so called war powers legislation, the central government has maintained that these military adventures are constitutional. Even worse, these costly campaigns have not been wars at all but rather have been never-ending skirmishes from which the U.S. eventually withdraws without victory.

The Constitution is crystal clear about war: only Congress has the power to declare it but through the fiction of war powers legislation, American lives have been squandered for nothing. This insane moral outrage must be stopped now.

Effect of Article 10

Ratification of an Amendment enacting this Article would put an end to all future American military adventures. So called war powers legislation would immediately be nullified because this specious legislation is based on the Congressional power to declare war. Removing the power to declare war from Congress would also mean that all current military adventures, such as Iraq and Afghanistan would have to be swiftly concluded.

In the event a real external military threat to the United States arose, the States could quickly adopt resolutions of war. Those resolutions would compel the U.S. to actually conduct war, not years and years of skirmishes. These resolutions would also contain the mission of the war by identifying in particular the enemy and by requiring that the threat from that enemy be eliminated.

No more could civilians like Robert McNamara and his team of "game theorists" from Yale and Princeton determine the military mission. Neither could a President fashion a mission to improve his politics or an expedient exit from war when the threat from the enemy had not been eliminated. The States would decide when the Republic was in danger and would declare war that is total: the threat from the identified enemy will be eliminated using all necessary acts of war.

The American TV audience would be removed as a weapon available to our enemies to shape the perception of the war. The enemy, the threat, and the definition of victory—the elimination of the threat by enemy—would all be defined in the declarations of war adopted by the States.

ARTICLE 11: Members Of Congress To Serve Single Term

FEDERAL POLITICAL CAREERS DIMINISHED: U.S. SENATORS AND MEMBERS OF THE HOUSE MAY SERVE ONLY ONE TERM

"No person shall serve as a United States Senator or a Member of the United States House of Representatives for more than one elected term; serving any portion of the vacated term of another person shall be deemed an elected term."

Need For Article 11

Federal political careerism is a major threat to the Republic. Federal career politicians have clearly and amply demonstrated that governance is their tertiary concern. Their primary goal is re-election and their secondary goal is to generate a path to office for one of their friends. If a federal politician could not have a career, and could only be elected to contribute to public policy, people of better character would be elected to Congress.

Effect of Article 11

Ratification of an Amendment enacting this Article would diminish federal political careers in America. Although not required by this article, diminishing federal political careers would give credence to the idea that the taxpayers do not need to provide pensions for folks who serve only once.

As an Amendment, this Article would make it clear to even the most crass political aspirant that governance, and preservation of the Republic, are serious things. Diminishing federal political careerism would go a long way towards sweeping the riffraff out of Washington.

ARTICLE 12: Congress Members May Serve In One House Only

FEDERAL POLITICAL CAREERS AND FEDERAL CRONYISM DIMINISHED: CONGRESSIONAL SERVICE LIMITED TO EITHER THE U.S. SENATE OR THE U.S. HOUSE

"No person who served any portion of an elected term, including a vacated term, as a United States Senator shall be candidate for, shall be elected as, or shall serve as a Member of the United States House of Representatives; no person who served any portion of an elected term, including a vacated term, as a Member of the United States House of Representatives shall be a candidate for, shall be elected as, or shall serve as a United States Senator."

Need For Article 12

This Article is needed to complement Article 11 in the diminishing of federal political careers in America. Otherwise, politicians seeking a career—rather than a contribution to the Republic—who would be blocked by Article 11 from serving more than one term in one house of Congress would simply switch to the other house of Congress.

Effect of Article 12

Ratification of an Amendment enacting this Article would prevent politicians from establishing federal political careers by switching from one house of Congress to the other house of Congress.

ARTICLE 13: Members Of Congress Excluded From Cabinet

FEDERAL POLITICAL CAREERS AND FEDERAL CRONYISM DIMINISHED: MEMBERS OF CONGRESS EXCLUDED FROM THE CABINET

"No person who served any portion of an elected term, including a vacated term, as a United States Senator or as a Member of the United States House of Representatives, shall serve in any capacity in any Cabinet of any President of the United States."

Need For Article 13

Currently, the primary goal of federal career politicians is to get reelected. Their secondary goal is to prepare a path to office for one of their friends, with the understanding that the newly elected or appointed friend will return the favor. This cronyism is antagonistic to the goal of office holders having a primary goal of making a contribution to governance.

Effect of Article 13

Ratification of an Amendment enacting this Article would break the cycle of cronyism that American presidents have perpetuated. The President would be forced to staff his cabinet with people who could contribute expertise rather than clubby connections.

ARTICLE 15: Ambassador Must First Be Secretary Of State In A State

COMPROMISE EXPERIENCE REQUIRED FOR DIPLOMACY: U.S. AMBASSADORS MUST FIRST SERVE AS SECRETARY OF STATE IN ONE OF THE STATES

"No person shall be appointed to or serve as a United States Ambassador who has not been previously elected to and served an elected term in the office of Secretary of State of one of the States."

Need For Article 15

Ambassadorships have always been plum patronage prizes. Senate approval is a mere formality and presidents have bestowed these vestiges of aristocratic living upon whomever they please. Ambassadors are not required to have actual experience in negotiation. Moreover, those who have served as Secretary of State in one of the States is not likely to confuse the role of negotiation in the presentation of policy with the role of making policy.

Effect of Article 15

Ratification of an Amendment enacting this Article would restrict the pool of future ambassadors to former Secretaries of States for the States. Presidents would likely form more cordial relationships with contemporary Secretaries of State for the States, whom they might need as ambassadors; as a result, the President's awareness of the importance of the State governments would be bolstered.

ARTICLE 16: President Must Be Born In A State

MAINTAINING THE INTEGRITY OF THE PRESIDENCY: U.S. PRESIDENT MUST BE BORN IN ONE OF THE STATES, DISTRICT OF COLUMBIA EXCLUDED FROM STATEHOOD

"No person shall be a candidate for, be elected to the office of, or shall serve as the President of the United States who was not born in one of the States. The District of Columbia is not a State, shall not become a State, and shall be directly and exclusively governed by the Congress of the United States."

Need For Article 16

Because the central government was created by the legislatures of the States to serve the legislatures of the States, the President should have been born in one of the States. Territories, possessions, and the District of Columbia, did not create the central government and should not be allowed to have one of their citizens become President.

Effect of Article 16

Ratification of an Amendment enacting this Article would ensure that candidates for, and those serving as, President were born in one of the States. The District of Columbia would be prevented from becoming a State and from governing itself.

ARTICLE 17: Treaty Inferior To US Law

FOREIGN ENTANGLEMENT DIMINISHED: TREATIES INFERIOR TO FEDERAL LAWS

"No portion of any provision of any treaty ratified by the United States Senate shall be considered superior to any portion of any United States law; any portion of any provision of any treaty ratified by the United States Senate that is contrary to, contravenes or restricts or diminishes the power of any United States law is null and void and has no force of law or precedent within the jurisdiction of the United States of America."

Need For Article 17

The threat to the Republic does not come only from those who want to impose an unconstitutional nationalist government by perverting principles asserted in the Constitution. There are those in America who want to subvert our sovereignty to foreign powers. This article helps maintain the sovereignty of the Republic.

Effect of Article 17

Ratification of an Amendment enacting this Article would immediately nullify any provision of any treaty that asserted superiority over any U.S. law. The ratification process would be forced to ensure that U.S. law was superior to each and every provision of each and every treaty.

ARTICLE 18: Birth Citizenship Restricted To Children Of US Citizens

ESTABLISHING INTEGRITY OF CITIZENSHIP: BIRTH CITIZENSHIP RESTRICTED TO CHILDREN OF CITIZENS

"No person shall become a United States citizen at birth unless, at the time of birth, that person's biological mother was already a United States citizen and that person's biological father was already a United States citizen."

Need For Article 18

States are the cornerstone of federal government. Their integrity must be asserted and protected at all times to preserve constitutional federal government. Citizenship is the keystone of State government. The integrity of citizenship must be asserted and protected at all times. The same forces in America that seek to destroy constitutional federal government by annihilating the States as holders of political power also seek to destroy the meaning of citizenship by granting it at birth to those whose parents illegally stood on the soil of one of the United States when having a baby.

Twenty five million illegal interlopers are already here and their kids will become citizens at birth unless this Article is enacted to prevent this travesty.

Effect of Article 18

Children born to the twenty five million interlopers already in the United States would not become citizens of the U.S. at birth. Citizenship at birth also would not be granted to those children who only had one parent who was already a valid U.S. citizen. Knowing that their kids could not become U.S. citizens just by being delivered on U.S. soil, many potential Illegal Interlopers would lose some of their incentive to flaunt U.S. law and invade our sovereign territory. Also, children would no longer be an anchor keeping illegals from being deported back to their own countries where they could avail themselves of the opportunity to improve their own societies.

ARTICLE 19: Legal Entry Required For Immigrant Citizenship

MAINTAINING INTEGRITY OF CITIZENSHIP: LEGAL ENTRY REQUIRED FOR IMMIGRANT CITIZENSHIP

"No person who was not a United States citizen at birth shall become a United States citizen if that person has ever entered the United States illegally; or if that person has ever been deported from the United States or its territories or possessions; or if that person has been convicted of a crime or misdemeanor in the United States or its territories or possessions; or if that person has participated in armed combat against the United States or its territories or possessions."

Need For Article 19

This Article is the true Dream Act. It will absolutely prevent a "path to citizenship" for the twenty five million illegal interlopers who are already in the United States.

Effect of Article 19

Ratification of an Amendment enacting this Article would be the true Dream Act. It would absolutely prevent a "path to citizenship" for the twenty five million illegal interlopers who are already in the United States. This Article would open the floodgates for the deportation of illegal interlopers back to their own countries where they could avail themselves of the opportunity to improve their own societies.

ARTICLE 20: Return To Gold Standard

PROTECTING THE VALUE OF THE CURRENCY: FIAT CURRENCY ABOLISHED, RETURN TO THE GOLD STANDARD, ABOLITION OF THE FEDERAL RESERVE

"Section1: The Federal Reserve Act of 1913, the Board of Governors of the Federal Reserve, and all Federal Reserve banks, are hereby abolished and shall receive no additional monies or credit from the government of the United States. The liabilities of the Federal Reserve shall be paid only from the assets of the Federal Reserve existing when this amendment is ratified.

Section 2: Congress shall enact no law establishing a fiat currency or any form of legal tender that is not redeemable in gold; Congress shall establish the value of the legal tender of the United States in gold and shall provide for the redemption of all legal tender of the United States in gold; no central bank shall be established for the United States and Congress shall directly coin, establish the value of, and manage the supply of all legal tender for the United States of America."

Need For Article 20

"Paper is poverty....it is only the ghost of money and not money itself."

Thomas Jefferson, letter to Colonel Edward Carrington

Since we left the gold standard and created the sleight-of-hand PRIVATE corporation known as the Federal Reserve, America has maintained a fiat currency and amassed trillions in debt. This debt will make us vassals to countries who generate actual wealth. This economic recklessness is a grave threat to the Republic and must be stopped in its tracks—now!

Effect of Article 20

Ratification of an Amendment enacting this Article would give America a currency secured by gold. The Federal Reserve would be eliminated. The U.S. Treasury would then have to sell its debt—and its credit worthiness—to actual investors. The central government's insatiable appetite for MINDLESS SPENDING TO BUY VOTES would be curbed because the government could NOT PRINT MONEY UNLESS IT HAD THE GOLD TO BACK IT UP. Central banks created the Great Depression. Eliminating ours will ensure that we don't inflict that misery upon the world again.

ARTICLE 21: Hate Speech Protected

PROTECTING THE INTEGRITY OF FREEDOM OF SPEECH: EXPRESSION OF HATRED IN SPEECH PROTECTED

"Section 1: Congress shall make no law abridging the freedom of the expression of hatred, disdain, opposition, reproach, ridicule or challenge in speech.

Section 2: Congress shall make no law establishing hatred as a crime, shall make no law establishing the motive of hatred as a crime, and shall make no law establishing the motive of hatred as basis for any punishment or exacerbation of punishment whatsoever."

Need For Article 21

"Let the human mind loose. It must be loose. It will be loose. Superstition and despotism cannot confine it."

John Adams

Hatred is vital to the Republic. Silencing hatred is but a deceptive way to begin silencing all dissent. This entire book is devoted to hatred of those people in America who would erode our Constitutional federal government into an illegal, unconstitutional nationalist government. Hatred in speech must be protected before we all fall victim to the pleasance of silence.

So-called "hate" crimes are not crimes at all. They are political repression enacted into legislation and this legislation needs to be invalidated and prevented in the future.

Effect of Article 21

Ratification of an Amendment enacting this Article would protect the expression of hatred in speech and nullify legislation attempting to restrict or ban "hate speech". This article would invalidate current "hate" crime legislation and prevent the formulation of new laws defining hate as a crime.

ARTICLE 22: Withdrawal From The United Nations

U.S. SOVEREIGNTY PROTECTED AND FOREIGN ENTANGLEMENTS DIMINISHED: U.S. MEMBERSHIP IN GLOBAL GOVERNANCE ORGANIZATIONS FORBIDDEN, MEMBERSHIP IN THE UNITED NATIONS WITHDRAWN

"Congress shall make no law nor ratify any treaty committing the United States to join associations of foreign nations or to contribute funds to associations of foreign nations that seek to regulate relations among nations or seek governance, in any form, over other nations."

Need For Article 22

There are those in America who want to subvert our sovereignty to foreign powers. Membership in the United Nations is one vehicle by which they would begin to cede American sovereignty to foreign powers or foreign organizations. Global governance in any form is an inherent evil and must be resisted at all turns. This article helps maintain the sovereignty of the Republic.

Effect of Article 22

Ratification of an Amendment enacting this Article would immediately terminate U.S. membership in the United Nations and prevent future membership in organizations which attempt to govern foreign countries.

ARTICLE 23: Abolition Of Federal Education

IMPROVEMENT OF EDUCATION: ABOLITION OF THE DEPARTMENT OF EDUCATION, FUNDING SCHOOL DISTRICTS UNEQUALLY OR VIA LOCAL PROPERTY TAXES FORBIDDEN; ABOLITION OF EDUCATIONAL CAREERISM, SUBJECT MASTER'S DEGREE REQUIRED OF ALL PUBLIC EDUCATORS AND ADMINISTRATORS

"Section 1: Congress shall make no law establishing a responsibility of the United States government for the education of the peoples in the States; Congress shall not create and shall not fund any office of the government of the United States for the purpose of directing, in any manner, the education of the peoples in the States.

Section 2: The government of the United States shall not employ or pay for the services of any person unless the State where that person resides at the time of engagement by the government of the United States requires by statute that the State's schools be funded equally from the general fund of the State's treasury; and that no person shall teach or administer in the State's schools who has not been awarded a Master's degree in a curriculum subject;

provided that the theory and practice of education shall not be deemed curriculum subjects."

Need For Article 23

Public school teaching is not a profession. We entrust our children to people who have achieved nothing other than a degree in the non-intellectual, non-academic, fabricated discipline of "Education". Requiring a Master's degree in an intellectual subject ensures that teachers have a mastery of the subject they aspire to teach. In addition, those who became teachers solely because "they love children" would be barred from teaching.

Funding schools from local property taxes has always been the wrong, illegal and unconstitutional way to provide for public education. This method is unconstitutional because every State constitution claims the State, not constituencies within the State, has the obligation for public education. Therefore, funding schools by property taxes is unconstitutional.

What is unconstitutional is by definition illegal. Consequently, funding schools by property taxes is illegal.

The State, as a political entity, does not have gradations so people in poor neighborhoods do not have less of a responsibility to fund public education than people in rich neighborhoods. Since everyone must bear the responsibility for public education, and the same education must be provided to all, funding schools by property taxes is wrong.

Effect of Article 23

Ratification of an Amendment enacting this Article would make teaching a legitimate profession, improve the qualifications of those charged with imparting knowledge to our children, and would provide more equal funding for all schools.

ARTICLE 24: Commerce Clause Restricted

CONGRESS AND THE U.S. SUPREME COURT RESTRAINED: COMMERCE CLAUSE LIMITED TO ACTUAL COMMERCE

"Article 1, Section 8, Clause 3 of this Constitution shall be construed only as giving Congress the power to regulate the reasonably free flow of goods and services among the States and no other power. The government of the United States shall not maliciously harm, by the flow of goods and services, the commerce of any State or the commerce of the United States."

Need For Article 24

The expansionist central government, and its prestige seeking handmaiden, the Supreme Court, have used the Commerce Clause of the Constitution to enhance their dominions at the expense of the sovereignty of the States and the liberties of the people. They will not stop themselves. They will not restore the proper meaning of the Commerce Clause. This Article will stop them cold.

Effect of Article 24

Ratification of an Amendment enacting this Article would prevent the Commerce Clause from being used in the future to expand the power of the central government or the prerogatives of the Supreme Court. This Article would also provide the immediate basis for appealing and overturning scores of Supreme Court decisions which have distorted the proper meaning of the Commerce Clause.

ARTICLE 25: Volunteer Service Abolished And Universal Conscription Established

U.S. MILITARY STRENGTHENED: VOLUNTEER SERVICE ABOLISHED, YOUTH SOLDIERING ABOLISHED, UNIVERSAL CONSCRIPTION OF CITIZENS ESTABLISHED, MILITARY SERVICE COMMITTED SOLELY TO COMBAT

"Section1: No person shall serve in the armed forces of the United States unless that person has been conscripted into service; volunteer entry into service in the armed forces of the United States is hereby abolished.

Section 2: No person between the ages of twenty-one years and twenty-four years shall be exempt from conscription into service in the armed forces of the United States; no person younger than twenty-one years and no person older than twenty-four years shall be conscripted into service in the armed forces of the United States.

Section 3: No person shall be conscripted into service in the armed forces of the United States who is not a citizen of the United States.

Section 4: No person conscripted into service in the armed forces of the United States shall serve in those armed forces unless deemed fit in the sole discretion of military authorities of those armed forces. All civilian authorities, including the Commander-in-chief, shall have no power to determine who is fit to serve in the armed forces of the United States or who serves in the armed forces of the United States.

Section 5: Every person conscripted into service and who serves in the armed forces of the United States shall serve only in the role of a combatant. All non-combatant services shall be provided to the armed forces of the United States by civilians, who shall not be deemed members of the armed forces of the United States and shall not receive military honors or military benefits."

Need For Article 25

The all-volunteer military is unconstitutional because the defense of the Constitution is the obligation of all citizens, not just those who volunteer. Non-citizens have no duty to defend the Constitution and therefore have no place in the armed forces of the United States. The defense of the Republic is too important to allow civilians to use social politics to determine who is fit to serve in the armed forces of the United States. Support service is not combat service and must be performed by civilians who are not eligible to receive military honors and benefits.

Effect of Article 25

Ratification of an Amendment enacting this Article would immediately end the all-volunteer military. The definition of who may serve in the armed forces would be returned to the military and put beyond the purview and politics of all civilians, including the Supreme Court and the President.

www.ingramcontent.com/pod-product-compliance
Lightning Source LLC
Chambersburg PA
CBHW062113080426
42734CB00012B/2841